fushigi yûgi™

The Mysterious Play
VOL. 10: ENEMY

Story & Art By
YUU WATASE

FUSHIGI YÛGI
THE MYSTERIOUS PLAY, VOL. 10: ENEMY
Gollancz Manga Edition

STORY AND ART BY YUU WATASE

English Adaptation/Yuji Oniki
Touch-Up & Lettering/Bill Spicer
Cover, Graphics & Design/Hidemi Sahara
Editor/William Flanagan
UK Cover Adaptation/Sue Michniewicz

This edition published in Great Britain in 2006 by Gollancz Manga,
an imprint of the Orion Publishing Group, Orion House, 5 Upper St Martin's Lane,
London WC2H 9EA, and a licensee of VIZ Media, LLC.

1 3 5 7 9 10 8 6 4 2

A CIP catalogue record for this book is available from the British Library

ISBN 0 57507 830 8
EAN 9780 57507 830 7

Printed and bound at Mackays of Chatham, PLC

PARENTAL ADVISORY
FUSHIGI YUGI is rated T+ for Teen Plus.
Contains sexual situations and realistic violence.
Recommended for older teens (16 and up).

www.orionbooks.co.uk

CONTENTS

STORY THUS FAR

Chipper junior-high-school girl Miaka is physically drawn into the world of a strange book—*The Universe of the Four Gods*. Miaka is offered the role of the lead character, the Priestess of the god Suzaku, and is charged with a mission to save the nation of Hong-Nan, and in the process have three wishes granted.

While Miaka makes a short trip back to the real world, her best friend Yui is sucked into the book only to suffer rape and manipulation, which drives her to attempt suicide. Now, Yui has become the Priestess of the god Seiryu, the bitter enemy of Suzaku and Miaka.

The only way for Miaka to gain back the trust of her former friend is to summon the god Suzaku and wish to be reconciled with Yui, so Miaka reenters the world of *The Universe of the Four Gods*. The Seiryu warriors ruin Miaka's first attempt to summon Suzaku, but the oracle, Tai Yi-Jun, has a new quest for Miaka and her Celestial Warriors of Suzaku—to obtain Shentso-Pao, treasures from the countries of the other two gods, Genbu and Byakko. Success will allow them to summon Suzaku. Only seconds after obtaining the first treasure, it is stolen from Miaka's hand by the Seiryu Warriors, leaving her wracked with guilt. Miaka, falling for a Seiryu trick, tries to get the treasure back, but instead is trapped by Nakago, who is intent on forcing sex on her. She is fully in his power as she falls unconscious. Later, Tamahome arrives to save her, inflicting a terrible wound on Nakago, but Tamahome's assurances aren't enough to calm Miaka's heart. She runs away from Tamahome, trips and sprains her ankle, and is immediately found by a Seiryu warrior wielding a deadly weapon!

The Universe of the Four Gods is based on ancient China, but Japanese pronunciation of Chinese names differs slightly from their Chinese equivalents. Here is a short glossary of the Japanese pronunciation of the Chinese names in this graphic novel:

CHINESE	JAPANESE	PERSON OR PLACE	MEANING
Xong Gui-Siu	Sô kishuku	Tamahome's Name	Demon Constellation
Hong-Nan	Konan	Southern Kingdom	Crimson South
Qu-Dong	Kutô	Eastern Kingdom	Gathered East
Bei-Jia	Hokkan	Northern Kingdom	Armored North
Xi-Lang	Sairô	Western Kingdom	West Tower
Shentso-Pao	Shinzahô	A Treasure	God's Seat Jewel
Tai Yi-Jun	Tai Itsukun	An Oracle	Preeminent Person

SUBOSHI !
I WON'T LET YOU GET AWAY.
YOU'LL NEVER LEAVE THIS PLACE ALIVE!!
OH, NO !!
WHAT'LL I DO !?
CHAPTER FIFTY-FIVE
ILLUSIONARY
WARMTH

CHAPTER FIFTY-FIVE
ILLUSIONARY WARMTH

?

NAKAGO

- He comes from an immigrant tribe of the far west.
- Commander of 2/3 of Qu-Dong's armed forces.
- No living family or friends.
- 25 years old.
- Height: 6' 4" (193 cm.)
- Ability: Chi attack techniques.
- Hobbies: Making Tamahome miserable (ha ha!).
- Personality: Beyond cold, he's Arctic ice! His name is a misnomer (a dwelling for the heart); his plans and actions show a complete lack of mercy. He allows for no emotional distraction nor wasted action. Once someone's usefulness is exhausted, the person is eliminated. On the other hand, he has an undeniable charisma which allows him to skillfully manipulate people. But what goes on in his mind remains a mystery.

HON GŌ YUI
本鄕唯

YUI

- Birth Place: Tokyo. Miaka's classmate, 15 years old.
- An only child. Latchkey kid -- both parents work.
- Height: 5' 3" (162 cm.)
- Weight: 108 lbs. (49 kg.)
- Vision: Right 20/18, Left 20/15
- Blood type: AB
- Hobbies: Reading (mysteries), music.
- Personality: In keeping with her looks, she is more mature than an average 15-year-old. Bold and confident in everything she does. Tends to see the world in black and white. Passionate, but passion turns to fury with betrayal. On the outside, she's supremely self-confident, but underneath, she longs for someone to take care of her.

I TWISTED MY ANKLE. I CAN'T MOVE!
HOW COULD SUBOSHI BE HERE!?
THIS IS IT FOR ME!

GET DOWN !!
WHA-- ?

WHA--
?
WHA--
!?
...ARE YOU ALL RIGHT!? IT WAS A GIANT POLECAT. IT WAS ABOUT TO *GET* YOU.
SUBOSHI
!?
ARE YOU OKAY? YOU NEED SOME HELP?
B--
BUT... WHY
?

H-HEY... ARE YOU ALL RIGHT !?
HM?
HUFF HUFF
DAMN... I CAN HIT SAND ALL I WANT, BUT IT WON'T DO MUCH FOR MY SKILLS.

Hello, it's me, Watase. I just pulled my first all-nighter in quite a while, so I'm totally zoning out... ZZZZ... Hey, wake up! No sleep for me!
I don't really have a theme for this column (how much of a theme can you have in a 1/3-page column like this?)... so I'll just write down whatever comes to my numb mind.
In this story, there's a concept called the 28 constellations. For those who haven't read FY serialized in Shōjo Comic, it had an issue with a supplementary chart of astrological fortunes based on the 28 constellations. Apparently, that was the first time a chart like that has ever appeared in Japan! I tried it, and it was really fun! According to the editor who wrote the text, it was from an Indian 27-constellation astrology system that made its way as far as China! The characters (y'know, my characters) like Chichiri and Tamahome had their own personalities and attributes which ended up corresponding to the historical charts! It really surprised me.
I think my star sign was one of the constellations in Byakko. *I forgot which one.* I read the astrologer's notes and it was so similar to my story. That was another surprise!
The "Eastern Seiryu" was the sea god representing the waters from which life springs. The "Northern Genbu" is the cycle of death and rebirth as represented by the turtle and snake. (As far as death goes, there's Nuriko and Hikitsu. And rebirth means you're reincarnated. Of course, that was just a coincidence.) The "Western Byakko" represents worship of holy mountains. Western China is surrounded by mountains. *And the sea is in the east. See?*

I TREATED HIM A LITTLE ON THE ROAD, BUT THE WOUND IS SEVERE.
WE'LL HAVE TO STAY HERE FOR A WHILE SO THAT YOU CAN RECOVER.
IMPOSSIBLE. WE MUST GET TO XI-LANG AS SOON AS WE CAN!
NOT WITH *THAT* WOUND! THAT'S AN ORDER!
AS YOU WISH.
IT'S LIKE YOUR ARM *MELTED!* WHO DID THAT TO YOU?
YOU DESERVE IT! NYAH! NYAH!
....

HUFF HUFF
MIAKA!!
MIAKA!!
MIAKA!!
MIAKA! WHERE DID YOU GO? WHY DID YOU LEAVE ME!?!
"I WON'T BE ABLE TO MARRY YOU ANYMORE."

HOW MUCH PAIN WILL SATISFY YOU ?
MY FAMILY...
...FRIENDS...
...AND THEN...
WHEN WILL YOU STOP TAKING FROM ME ALL THE THINGS I LOVE, NAKAGO !?!
MEOW! MEOW!! MEOW !!
MIAKA'S EYES AREN'T SO SQUINTY!
REALLY? I THOUGHT IT WAS PRETTY GOOD!

"...MIAKA..."
HM ...
"COME HERE."
"WO AI NI."

TAMA-HOME ...
AH!
WE'RE FINALLY BOUND TO EACH OTHER!
FINALLY...
OH, NO!
DON'T !

NOOOO!
HEY! ARE YOU ALL RIGHT !?
GOOD... YOU'RE FINALLY AWAKE!
OH, YEAH!
DON'T WORRY. YOU'RE IN MY HOUSE IN THE VILLAGE OF MUOHAN NEAR THE XI-LANG BORDER.
!
YOU WERE OUT FOR THREE DAYS.
YOU MUST HAVE BEEN PRETTY DARN TIRED.
YOU'RE RIGHT, I WAS.
SO YOU'RE... NOT SUBOSHI, ARE YOU? WHY DID YOU...

ME? I'M...
バタバタ
WHAT IS IT, HUAIKE !?
OH! YOU'RE AWAKE, YOUNG LADY!
DOES YOUR LEG STILL HURT?
OH! NO, IT DOESN'T HURT AT ALL.
OF COURSE IT DOESN'T! WE GAVE YOU A POTION WITH THE "OBLIVION HERB."
THE BEST HEALER IN THE VILLAGE MADE IT. YOU EVEN FORGET YOU WERE EVER IN PAIN!
BUT IF YOU TAKE TOO MUCH, IT CAN *KILL* YOU. IT'S REALLY POTENT STUFF!

A FLUTE !?
BUT NOW YOU SHOULD RELAX AND GET MORE REST.
HUAIKE, YOUR FLUTE IS SO SOOTHING. PLAY A TUNE FOR HER.
YES, OF COURSE.
AMIBOSHI ...
HE'S AMIBOSHI !!
THIS SONG... IT *HAS* TO BE HIM!
AMIBOSHI... SUBOSHI'S OLDER TWIN BROTHER, AND THE SEIRYU WARRIOR WHO TRICKED US. HE FELL INTO THE RIVER, BUT I THOUGHT HE DROWNED IN THE RAPIDS.

BUT HE'S STILL ALIVE!
THEY CALLED HIM HUAIKE... DOES HE HAVE AMNESIA? HE DOESN'T SEEM TO REMEMBER ME AT ALL.
A SEIRYU WARRIOR... *HERE* OF ALL PLACES...
ONE OF NAKAGO'S COMPANIONS.
I WONDER IF MY DREAM WILL EVER COME TRUE...
TAMAHOME ...
BUT WE'LL NEVER MEET AGAIN.
NEVER ...

EVERYTHING IS PROCEEDING EXACTLY AS PLANNED. WITH THE EXCEPTION OF TAMAHOME, OF COURSE...
NOW THAT THE PRIESTESS OF SUZAKU HAS LOST HER VIRGINITY, ALL THAT IS LEFT IS TO OBTAIN THE SHENTSO-PAO OF XI-LANG, AND...
IS THAT YOU, TOMO?
WHAT-EVER HAPPENED TO YOU, NAKAGO?
HOW UNUSUAL TO SEE YOU WOUNDED.
OF COURSE SHE IS, IT IS SIMPLY--
THE PRIESTESS OF SUZAKU IS STILL A VIRGIN.
I DID NOT HAVE INTER-COURSE WITH THE PRIESTESS OF SUZAKU.
WHAT DID YOU SAY?

JUST WHEN I...
!!
A BRIGHT RED FLAME CAME BURSTING FROM THE PRIESTESS' BODY.
HER BARRIER WAS PERFECT. IT WAS IMPOSSIBLE TO EVEN TOUCH HER. HER POWER TOOK ME BY SURPRISE.
YOU? *YOU!?* SURELY YOU COULD HAVE FOUND *SOME* WAY TO BREAK PAST THE LITTLE GIRL'S PROTECTIVE BARRIER!
SHE MAY LOOK FRAIL, BUT SHE *IS* A PRIESTESS. BESIDES, I HAD NO DESIRE TO SLEEP WITH A COMATOSE BODY.
BUT IT WAS A PERFECT OPPOR-TUNITY!

THE GIRL BELIEVES SHE'S BEEN DEFILED... JUST AS HER EMINENCE YUI BELIEVES.
IF THE RESULTS ARE THE SAME, WHAT MATTERS THE METHODS ?
NAKAGO... PERHAPS YOU DIDN'T VIOLATE THE PRIESTESS BECAUSE YOU SAW IN HER... A LITTLE OF YOURSELF?
MY APOLOGIES. I SHOULD HAVE REMEMBERED THAT SUBJECT IS TABOO.
VERY WELL. I SHALL TAKE CARE OF THE PRIESTESS OF SUZAKU.
HOWEVER, FIRST, I MUST DEAL WITH TAMA-HOME...

SOI!
TO SERVE WHAT I HAVE COOKED FOR TAMAHOME, I REQUIRE SOI'S HELP. I KNOW WHERE HE IS.
NAKAGO, DO YOU APPROVE?
DO AS YOU LIKE.
WE SHOULD PUT THOSE WRITHING, WOUNDED SUZAKU CHICKS OUT OF THEIR MISERY.
ポムッ
THAT DOES IT!

MOM, WE MADE BREAKFA--
YOU LOOK WONDERFUL.
THE CLOTHES I WORE AS A GIRL FIT PERFECTLY ON YOU!
UMM... MY SCHOOL UNIFORM...
OH, IT NEEDS SOME FIXING. IT MIGHT TAKE A WHILE BECAUSE OF THE ODD FABRIC.
WHAT DO YOU THINK, HUAIKE?
WOW!
YOU SURE LOOK *CUTE!*
I WONDER WHAT TAMAHOME WOULD SAY ...

HERE, EAT UP!
BUT...
YESTERDAY, YOU WENT WITHOUT. YOU HAVE TO *EAT* TO BUILD UP STRENGTH.
THAT'S TRUE, HUH?
YES, YES.
カラン
...I'LL JUST HAVE A BITE.
UMPH!
AHHHHHH!
ON SECOND THOUGHT, A STARVED BODY SHOULD TAKE IT A *LITTLE* AT A TIME!
YOU'RE RIGHT, IF I DON'T EAT...
モシャ モシャ
...IT'S BAD FOR ME, SO...
YOU THINK SO?
PHEW!!!

I HEARD SOMETHING ABOUT A JOURNEY, MIAKA ?
WHERE ARE YOU GOING ONCE YOUR LEGS ARE HEALED?
.....
LET'S SEE...
I DIDN'T PLAN THIS. WHAT'LL I DO NOW?
I CAN'T BE WITH TAMAHOME, BUT I GUESS THAT CHICHIRI AND THE OTHERS WON'T ACCEPT ME EITHER.
OF COURSE YOU COULD ALWAYS STAY AND BE HUAIKE'S *BRIDE*.
SPIT SPIT
DAD! MOM!
HEY! YOU'RE THE RIGHT AGE!
YOU WENT TO KILL THE POLECAT, AND AFTER YOU DID, YOU BROUGHT BACK THIS FINE, YOUNG GIRL... WHAT ELSE WOULD WE THINK?
STOP IT! I'M NOT EVEN *THINKING* OF A BRIDE RIGHT NOW!
...BRIDE ?

"I'LL MAKE YOU..."
"...THE HAPPIEST BRIDE IN THE WORLD."
IT WAS OUR PROMISE.
BUT...
...NO MORE.

MIAKA! I-I'M S-SORRY. I DIDN'T MEAN TO MAKE YOU CRY.
OH, NO. IT'S NOT YOU. *I'M* SORRY!
I'M GOING TO MY ROOM. DON'T WORRY, I'D JUST LIKE TO BE ALONE.
EVERYTHING I SEE OR HEAR JUST MAKES ME SAD.
LET'S GO...
...OUTSIDE!
D-DON'T BOTHER WITH ME--
IT'S BEAUTIFUL OUT THERE!
BEING COOPED UP IN HERE WON'T HELP YOU. I'LL BE YOUR FEET.

I DON'T WANT TO DO ANY--
WHOAH!
MOM, DAD, THE LADY AND I ARE GOING FOR A WALK!
not listening.
HEY! PUT ME DOWN !!
THEY LOOK SO GOOD TOGETHER.
YUP! YUP!
COME ON!! LET ME DOWN! I'M NOT IN THE MOOD!
AMIBO-- I MEAN... HUAIKE!

I DON'T THINK AMIBOSHI WAS EVER THIS FORWARD!
HE'S NOT HOW I REMEMBER!
YOUNG LADY ...
HERE, HAVE A PEACH.
EH?
IT'S YOU, HUAIKE!
IS *THIS* THE GIRL WHO WAS ATTACKED BY THE GIANT POLECAT?
THANK GOODNESS YOUR WOUNDS WERE ONLY MINOR.
ワイ ワイ
COME BY AND VISIT!
WE HAVE SOME DELICIOUS CINNAMON TEA.
HOW ADORABLE YOU LOOK IN THE CLOTHES FROM OUR VILLAGE! BUT YOU'RE NOT WEARING THE TRADITIONAL HAT!
I CAN'T BUY IT! I DON'T HAVE MONEY!
HA HA!
THEY DON'T WANT MONEY. THEY'RE JUST BEING FRIENDLY.

HEY, WHERE ARE YOU GOING?
I WANT TO CHECK ON THOSE TWO.
THERE YOU GO AGAIN. YOU WORRIED YOURSELF SICK WHEN HE WENT AFTER THE POLECAT.
ISN'T THIS TREE AMAZING? THIS IS MY FAVORITE PLACE!
I'M SORRY TO DRAG YOU OUT.
BUT I COULDN'T JUST LET YOU LIE THERE.
I WON'T ASK WHAT HAPPENED...
...BUT YOU SHOULDN'T WITHDRAW LIKE THAT.

PEOPLE ALWAYS DO THIS. ONE THING BAD HAPPENS, AND SUDDENLY EVERYTHING IN THE WORLD TURNS EVIL TO THEM.
THEN NEXT THING YOU KNOW, THINGS REALLY *DO* TURN BAD. YOU LOSE HOPE.
I DIDN'T WANT THAT TO HAPPEN FOR *YOU,* SO...
IT'S FINE FOR *YOU!* ISN'T IT, *AMIBOSHI !?!*
YOU JUST FORGET EVERY-THING!!
IT'S NOT *FAIR* TO LECTURE ME!

MY COMPANIONS, PEOPLE I LOVE...
...EVEN MY BEST FRIEND! THEY'RE ALL GONE.
I'VE HAD TERRIBLE THINGS HAPPEN AROUND ME AND TO ME, AND I CAN'T FORGET! FORGETTING WOULD BE A RELIEF!
AND YOU! YOU GET A PEACEFUL VILLAGE, LOVING FAMILY AND NICE NEIGHBORS! IT'S NOT FAIR!!
AND YOU GET TO FORGET WHAT YOU DID TO US.
THE PAIN THAT YOU INFLICTED ON US! YOU DON'T REMEMBER ANYTHING!

I'M SORRY.
I WAS UPSET, AND I TOOK YOU FOR SOMEONE ELSE! YOU'RE NOT AMIBOSHI.
GASP
.....
I JUST HAVE NO IDEA WHAT I'M SUPPOSED TO DO. I CAN'T EVEN THINK STRAIGHT.
DON'T LET WHAT I SAID BOTHER YOU.
!

THIS SONG !
IT'LL GIVE YOU STRENGTH AND COURAGE.
THANK YOU.
....

SKREE
HEY, CHICHIRI! THEY'RE FEEDIN' US LIKE *KINGS* AGAIN!
WHERE ARE MITSUKAKE AND CHIRIKO?
OH, THEM?
CHIRIKO'S GLUED TO TH' BOOKS DOWN-STAIRS.
AND MITSUKAKE FOUND SOME GREAT HEALIN' HERBS TO STUDY!
SKR EEE
WOULD YOU LIKE SOME MORE WINE, SIR?
HUH? YA *SURE* IT AIN'T NO PROBLEM? HELL YEAH!

MAN! I NEVER SEEN SUCH NICE FOLKS LIVIN' IN SUCH A NICE HOUSE!
WHO'DA THOUGHT XI-LANG WOULD TURN OUT T' BE SO GREAT!
IT *IS* NICE, BUT...
I WONDER WHY MIAKA AND TAMAHOME STILL HAVEN'T ARRIVED. NO DA.
I'VE BEEN TRYING TO REPORT BACK TO HIS MAJESTY, BUT SOMETHING IS INTERFERING. NO DA.
ELEPHANT EARS
DRAGONFLY
...
MIAKA'S TWIN BUN HAIR STYLE!
DID YA SAY SOME-THIN', CHICHIRI?
ONLY THAT I'LL *NEVER* HAVE A SERIOUS CON-VERSATION WITH YOU AGAIN! NO DA!
BUST LINE
WHAT IS THAT?

I USED MY "SHEN" SHELL TO CREATE AN ILLUSION OF XI-LANG FOR THE SUZAKU WARRIORS.
THEY'LL BURN IN THE MID-DAY SUN, AT NIGHT THEY'LL FREEZE. IN NO TIME, THEY'LL DIE OF EXPOSURE STRANDED IN THE DESERT LIKE THIS.
THEN WHY AM I HERE?
SOI, YOU ARE FAMILIAR WITH BEDDING TECHNIQUES. THROUGH SEX, YOU CAN CONTROL A MAN'S CHI.
YOU SAID THAT TAMAHOME'S CHI WOUNDED NAKAGO. THAT MEANS THE SUZAKU WARRIOR IS GETTING STRONGER.
LET'S USE YOUR TECHNIQUE TO RUIN ALL THAT.
I'M HOME!

SORRY I TOOK SO LONG.
I'LL GO DRAW SOME WATER.
URK!
O-OH! WEL-COME BACK!
MIAKA.
I'M SORRY FOR CRYING AND CARRYING ON!
O-OH, NO! IT'S QUITE ALL RIGHT. HERE, HAVE SOME SOUP. IT'S GOOD FOR YOU!
OH! THANK YOU!
AHHH!
IT'S DELICIOUS!

I... HUH?
MY BODY... FEELS HOT ALL OF THE SUDDEN...
THAT'S...
...STRANGE...
AH...
MIAKA!?

URR NNN ...
HUFF
HUFF
YOU FED HER THE OBLIVION HERB!? HOW COULD YOU!?
I WANTED HER TO FORGET ABOUT HUAIKE'S PAST!
IF SHE MADE YOU REMEMBER YOUR PAST, YOU'D GO AWAY AND LEAVE US FOREVER!
I DIDN'T REALIZE THAT I USED TOO MUCH. I DIDN'T!
CAN YOU EVER FORGIVE ME!?
DON'T BE FOOLISH, MOTHER. YOU TWO SAVED ME FROM DROWNING IN THE RIVER! HOW COULD I LEAVE YOU WHEN I OWE MY LIFE!?

FATHER, PLEASE GO AND CALM MOTHER DOWN.
I'LL TAKE CARE OF MIAKA.
HUFF HUFF HUFF
THIS IS NO GOOD. IF SHE'S ALLOWED TO STAY THIS HOT...
HUFF HUFF
...AHOME.
TAMA-HOME ...

TAMA-
HOME
...
I DON'T KNOW IF THIS WILL BRING DOWN A FEVER, BUT I HAVE TO TRY SOMETHING!

...TAMA...
...HOME...
?
I THOUGHT I HEARD SOMEONE CALL ME...
IT'S PROBABLY JUST THE HEAT.

YOU AGAIN? NO MORE IMPRESSIONS, OKAY? MY HORSE COLLAPSED, BUT YOU'RE STILL FINE...
MIAKA !?!
TAMA-HOME ...
MI--
MIAKA !!

I'VE BEEN LOOKING ALL OVER FOR YOU!! I'M GLAD YOU'RE SAFE!
SOI, TAMAHOME IS NOW UNDER THE SPELL. THE REST, I LEAVE TO YOU.
ぎゅっ
DON'T *EVER* DO THAT AGAIN, MIAKA!
HE SEES YOU AS THE PRIESTESS OF SUZAKU.
....
HA HA HA HA!
I'M PLACING HIM IN THE ARMS OF HIS BELOVED. YOU MIGHT CALL IT AN ACT OF KINDNESS.
TAMA-HOME.
I'M SO SORRY ...

TAMA-
HOME?
NO.
HE DOESN'T SMELL LIKE THIS.
THIS ISN'T TAMA-HOME.
!?
LET ME GO...
...NO !!
NO !!
MIAKA !?
SHE'S GOING INTO CONVUL-SIONS !

I FEEL...
AMI-BOSHI'S CHI...
?

WHAT'S THIS ?
SOME-THING'S ENTERING THROUGH MY MOUTH... ?

IS THIS...
A WARM FEELING, THROUGH MY WHOLE BODY!
...CHI?
!
AMI-BOSHI...? I...
YOUR FEVER'S DOWN.
!!
THANK GOOD-NESS!

!!
I'M... SORRY. I'M OUT OF STRENGTH...
CAN I STAY HERE... FOR A WHILE?
I CAN NEVER STAY AWAY FROM *YOU,* TAMA-HOME.
WHAT IS GOING ON?
TAMA-HOME'S THE ONLY ONE I WANT TO TOUCH ME LIKE THIS...
...BUT I CAN'T MOVE!

I'M SO SCARED... PLEASE HOLD ME TIGHT.
SO TIGHT EVERYTHING ELSE SLIPS AWAY...
MIAKA...
LET'S STAY TOGETHER...
LET'S LIVE HERE FOREVER!

CHAPTER FIFTY-SIX
DAWN FOR THE
HEART

AH!
AMIBOSHI... I MEAN HUAIKE...
...WHAT ARE YOU SAYING !?
"LET'S STAY TOGETHER..."
AS LONG AS YOU'RE HERE...
"LET'S LIVE HERE FOREVER!"
AS LONG AS YOU'RE HERE, THE WORLD CAN'T HURT YOU ANYMORE!

THIS IS A PEACEFUL VILLAGE. THEY'RE ALL NICE PEOPLE.
YOU'LL BE SAFE AS LONG AS YOU'RE HERE. AND MOTHER AND FATHER WOULD BE DELIGHTED.
IF I'M HERE...
...THE WORLD CAN'T...
...HURT ME.
GASP !!
OH, NO!
TAMA-HOME!

YOUR SKIN IS PERFECT.
BUT IT'S ON THE *INSIDE* THAT YOU'RE ALL TORN UP.
TAMA-HOME !!
S-S-STOP! O-OR I'LL...
...I'LL BITE OFF MY NOSE AND BLEED TO DEATH !!
EH?
ISN'T THE OLD THREAT, "I'LL BITE OFF MY *TONGUE*"?
!

YOUR FEVER'S DOWN. TAKE ANOTHER DAY TO REST UP.
ALSO, TAKE THE DAY TO THINK ABOUT WHAT I SAID.
LIVE HERE FOR-EVER ?
....

WHAT'S WRONG ?
OH... MY BODY SUDDENLY FEELS SO HOT...
THAT'S WEIRD.
IT MUST BE THE HEAT. LET'S GO INSIDE AND REST...
MI...AKA ?

NICE WORK. YOU PUT AN APHRODISIAC ON YOUR LIPS.
SUCH WORK COMES NATURALLY TO AN EXPERIENCED PROSTITUTE.
パサ パサッ
OH, NO!
NOW, AS YOU HALLUCINATE AN EMBRACE WITH YOUR BELOVED PRIESTESS...
...SOI WILL USE THE BEDDING TECHNIQUE TO DRIVE YOU INSANE AND LEAVE YOU TO ROT IN THE DESERT.
HA HA HA HA HA HA!

SUBOSHI!
THAT CHI...DID YOU FEEL IT?
YEAH... THAT WAS MY BROTHER'S. THAT'S *AMI-BOSHI'S* CHI!
BUT... I HEAR NO FLUTE.
WHEN HIS CHI IS RELEASED, IT'S THROUGH HIS MOUTH. LONG AGO I HAD A HIGH FEVER, AND HE REPLENISHED ME DIRECTLY WITH HIS CHI... BUT NORMALLY HE USED HIS FLUTE.
WHEN THE HECK?
I SEE. OF COURSE!
I NOW KNOW THE LOCATION...
...OF THE PRIESTESS OF SUZAKU.

UUNNNH...
NO!
!!
MY NECK...
...HURTS.
I HAD ANOTHER DREAM ABOUT NAKAGO.
HOW LONG AM I SUPPOSED TO SUFFER THROUGH THESE?
MIAKA?
CAN WE COME IN?
I'M SO SORRY, MIAKA.

(Continued)...

Now to continue with the southern Suzaku constellations.

The South had a symbolic meaning for the ancient Chinese emperor. While the Heavenly Ruler (Tai Yi-Jun) took care of the heavens, the earthly emperor was to rule the world from his throne in the south. *H-how lucky can Hotohori get?* The symbol for the South, the character for "Su" in Suzaku, represented the holy power of eternal life. In other words, the bird of eternal life (the Hōō, firebird or Phoenix). Amazingly, it was thought that once Suzaku was summoned, eternal peace would reign over the land!! Is that true, China!? That's the plot of Fushigi Yûgi! I was shocked!

Later this "North Star 28 Constellation Astrology" was applied, not only to the national interests, but to individuals as well. Suzaku guides the fates of love (with the name Hōō, the "Hō" part is male, and the "ō" part is female). So the Chinese people used to pray for love to the Suzaku constellations in the south. *Best of luck!*

By the way, I had no idea this kind of astrology even existed in Ancient China. It shocked the heck out of me!

Or maybe it was no coincidence that I chose the Suzaku for Miaka! L-Love? Well, I suppose.

Also, when I began this story, I came up with the characters and assigned each of them to constellations. But much to my surprise, when I casually looked up their meanings, I discovered (this really bowls me over!) that many of the stars corresponded to the characters' personalities!

To be continued...

I KNOW I DON'T HAVE THE RIGHT TO ASK AFTER WHAT I DID, BUT I WISH YOU WOULD STAY.
HUAIKE IS REALLY TAKEN BY YOU. IF YOU COULD SEE IT IN YOUR HEART...
OH, AND I MENDED AND WASHED YOUR CLOTHES... I HOPE YOU NEVER HAVE TO WEAR THEM THOUGH. PLEASE STAY HERE INSTEAD.
STAY HERE FOR-EVER.
I'LL NEVER SEE TAMAHOME AGAIN...
I'LL NEVER SUMMON SUZAKU. I HAVE NOWHERE ELSE TO GO.

YUI !
"MIAKA!! WHY DON'T YOU *ANSWER* ME-- !??"
YUI ENTERED THE WORLD OF THE BOOK TO RESCUE ME AND ENDED UP GETTING ATTACKED INSTEAD.
I THINK I UNDERSTAND YOU NOW. YOUR SADNESS. YOUR RESENTMENT... YOUR HATE. I KNOW NOW WHY YOU AIMED YOUR HATRED AT ME.
NOW THAT THE SAME THING HAPPENED TO ME, I UNDERSTAND.

I WONDER WHAT IT FELT LIKE. NAKAGO TELLING HER THAT I BETRAYED HER *EVERY DAY.*
I DIDN'T KNOW. I DIDN'T UNDERSTAND ANYTHING.
MIAKA.
はっ
HOW DO YOU FEEL?
スッ
HERE.
IT'S OBLIVION HERB.
TAKE A SIP, AND YOU'LL FORGET EVERY-THING.

...MIAKA...
MIAKA!!

MEOW, MYAA, ***MEOW!*** (...BUT THIS IS WHO SHE ***REALLY*** IS!)

GET IT? GET IT?

MEOW, ME-***MEOW!*** (TAMAHOME, SHE MAY ***LOOK*** LIKE MIAKA...)

...

NOTE: THE CAT ISN'T UNDER THE SPELL.

OH, NO!

OH, NO!

OH, NO!

MIAKA...

IF ONLY I COULD SPEAK THEIR DUMB LANGUAGE!

I ***KNEW*** IT WOULDN'T WORK.

I DO TOO.

I LOVE YOU.

I LOVE YOU ...
WHILE YOU DRINK, CONCENTRATE AND SAY, "I WANT TO FORGET EVERY-THING."
AND YOU WON'T SUFFER ANYMORE! IT'S *BEST* FOR YOU!
GIVE IT A TRY.
IF I DRINK THIS...
...MY SUFFERING WILL BE OVER.

MY PAIN...
...CAN BE FOR-GOTTEN!
I'LL FORGET IT ALL? NURIKO'S DEATH? THE OTHER WARRIORS?
YUI? AND...
...THE MAN WHO STILL LOVES ME DESPITE EVERYTHING. TAMAHOME!
I'M GOING TO FORGET THEM ALL!?

.....
... TAMA-HOME? WHAT'S WRONG ?

I CAN'T.
I WANT TO...
...BUT NOT NOW.
WH-- WHY !?
YOU HAVEN'T SUMMONED SUZAKU YET.
B-BUT NAKAGO TOOK ME ALREADY... I'VE BEEN DEFILED...
NO... I DON'T BELIEVE IT.
I DON'T KNOW HOW TO SAY THIS, BUT IF WE GIVE UP OUR WISHES, IF WE GIVE UP OUR HOPES, THEN ALL REALLY WILL BE LOST!
IF THERE IS EVEN A SLIVER OF A CHANCE ...

I BELIEVE IN YOU...
...MIAKA!
WHY?
DON'T YOU *WANT* YOUR SUFFERING TO END!?
I... I *CAN'T* FORGET!

THEY'RE PEOPLE WHO LOVE ME!! THEY'VE SAVED MY LIFE!! I CARE FOR THEM!
I CAN'T ALLOW MYSELF TO FORGET THEM !!
IS ONE OF THEM TAMAHOME? WHAT ABOUT HIM? DIDN'T YOU PROMISE TO NEVER LEAVE HIM ?
EH?
WHAT-- WHAT DID YOU JUST SAY !?
D-DO YOU...

I REMEMBER EVERYTHING. I AM A SEIRYU CELESTIAL WARRIOR.
YOUR ENEMY.
YES.
AMI... BOSHI !
WHY!? WHY DID YOU FAKE AMNESIA !?
I FELL INTO THE RIVER ON PURPOSE.
I WANTED TO DIE.

WHEN I BECAME A SPY POSING AS CHIRIKO AND LIVING AS A SUZAKU WARRIOR...
...I FELT THAT IT WAS A MISTAKE.
UNLIKE HONG-NAN, MY HOMELAND QU-DONG IS IN A STATE OF CONSTANT CIVIL STRIFE... MY BROTHER SUBOSHI AND I WERE ORPHANS.
WHEN HER EMINENCE YUI APPEARED FROM THE OTHER WORLD, I FIRMLY BELIEVED THAT ONCE SEIRYU WAS SUMMONED, QU-DONG WOULD FIND PEACE.
NAKAGO INSISTED THAT YOUR SUMMONING OF SUZAKU WOULD PREVENT THAT PEACE.
NAKAGO!
BUT THEN I REALIZED... THAT QU-DONG'S INTENTIONS WERE TO USE SEIRYU TO DOMINATE NOT ONLY HONG-NAN, BUT BEI-JIA AND XI-LANG AS WELL.
!!

AS I FELL INTO THE RIVER, I THOUGHT THAT MY DEATH WOULD PREVENT THE SUMMONING OF SEIRYU. I WAS JUST FED UP WITH FIGHTING.
I DIDN'T KNOW WHAT TO BELIEVE IN ANYMORE... AS A SEIRYU WARRIOR, I HAD NO CHOICE BUT TO FIGHT YOU.
IF THAT WERE TRUE, THE WAR WOULD KILL COUNTLESS NUMBERS OF PEOPLE.
THERE IS A WAY TO SUMMON SUZAKU AND SEIRYU, EVEN WITHOUT ALL THE CELESTIAL WARRIORS PRESENT.
THEN STAY HERE! WE WON'T HAVE TO FIGHT ANYMORE !!
WAR IS *POINTLESS!!* MIAKA, YOU THINK SO TOO, RIGHT !?
WHAT !?

YUI IS BEING USED!
"HER EMINENCE WAS NEVER RAPED."
NAKAGO IS DECEIVING HER SO HE CAN RULE THE WORLD !!
"YUI LOVES YOU."
"SO YOU MUST HELP HER."
"NO DA."
I HAVE TO GO!
GO!? WHERE ?
TO WHEREVER NAKAGO IS. I HAVE TO RESCUE YUI!
I'M CHANGING MY CLOTHES SO TURN AWAY.

NO, I'VE GOT A BETTER IDEA... I'LL HAVE YUI SUMMON SEIRYU!
WHAT !?
I CAN'T SUMMON SUZAKU ANYMORE. BUT SEIRYU CAN BE SUMMONED, RIGHT !?
IF YUI REALIZED HOW NAKAGO WAS DECEIVING HER, SHE'D UNDER-STAND! AFTER THAT SHE'D NEVER LISTEN TO NAKAGO OR THE QU-DONG RULERS!
YOU MAY BE RIGHT ABOUT THAT, BUT...
YOU'RE GOING ALONE? RIGHT INTO THE ENEMY'S CAMP? AREN'T YOU AFRAID!?
A LONG TIME AGO, SOMEBODY TOLD ME...
...THE KANJI CHARACTERS FOR "BATTLE" AND "RUNNING AWAY" DIFFER BY ONLY A FEW LINES...AND YET THEIR MEANINGS ARE EXACTLY OPPOSITE.
IF YOU RUN AWAY BECAUSE YOU "CAN'T DO IT" OR BECAUSE YOU THINK SOMETHING'S "IMPOSSIBLE"... THEN YOU'LL BECOME A COWARD AS AN ADULT.

SURE, I'M AFRAID! I'D LOVE TO RUN! BUT BECOMING A COWARD ISN'T IN MY PLANS!
SO I WON'T RUN. I'LL BATTLE IT THROUGH!
DON'T WORRY. YOU DON'T HAVE TO LEAVE HERE. I'LL GO ALONE!
MY ANKLE SEEMS FINE TOO.
BUT... ...WHY ?
BUT... ...WHY ?

I DON'T BELIEVE THIS! IT'S MY MOST POWERFUL APHRODISIAC, YET HE'S IN CONTROL!
HOW CAN HE DO IT?
IS THIS MAN...
...SO MUCH IN *LOVE* WITH THE PRIESTESS OF SUZAKU !?
SOI, YOU FAILED.
PERHAPS YOUR SEDUCTION SKILLS HAVE ATROPHIED.
WHO ARE YOU !?

MY NAME IS TOMO. AND I'M SORRY TO SAY...
...THAT YOU, TAMAHOME, SHALL NOW DIE.
I HAVE TO FIND YUI, NO MATTER WHAT!
GETTING HER TO SEE THAT I'M A FRIEND WON'T BE EASY. BUT THE ONLY WAY OUT OF THIS IS TO SUMMON SEIRYU. I'LL NEVER LET NAKAGO HAVE HIS WAY!
WE'LL SUMMON SEIRYU TO BRING PEACE TO THE WORLD.
THEN WE'LL GO HOME... TO OUR HOME.
WE'LL BE NORMAL JUNIOR HIGH SCHOOL KIDS, TAKING OUR ENTRANCE EXAMS, ENTERING HIGH SCHOOL.
THAT'S BEST. EVERYTHING WILL BE RESOLVED. IT'LL BE OVER.

AND THE LOVE BETWEEN TAMAHOME AND I...
...WILL ALSO END.
NOOOOO!!
AAAHHHH!!!
WH- WHAT IS IT !?
!!
HUAIKE'S PARENTS !!

From Volume 7 (Ah, the memories!)

I'LL HOLD YOU UNTIL YOU'RE FINISHED ...
URGH.
......
SUBOSHI ...
I WANNA DO THAT !

Long Overdue - Fushigi Akugi The Malicious Play (8)

The idea came from several readers ... I-I still don't know your names! Sorry! ♡

Are you that jealous, Nakago? Then why don't you cuddle up with Tamahome ... (krak)

Thank you for sending me all those dōjinshi and tapes, Ms. Haruta (great parody!). It was all really interesting! The Tasuki novel and the notebook with all your friends' drawings! I also received a "Ranma 1/2" video and cute illustrations from someone who is now an animator. I'd like to have all the fan art and character portraits from you readers displayed somewhere. Can I?

Why am I always in these dōjinshi !?

It never ends! They call me Akago, Inago, Mukago, Chicago ...

BGM: Final Fantasy IV (3 CD set)

There were so many others I received. Even ones that had love letters (?) to Fushigi characters. Everyone was so thrilled! There was one that was called "Nuriko in Heaven." A note to the fan who sent a gift to Mitsukake, in the CD Book II, he talks a lot more than he does in the manga. In fact he even laughs.

The names of each celestial warrior were written on each of these handmade chocolates!

The box was home made too.

Seven Celestial Chocolates

Tamahome Love

12 cm diameter.

2-3 cm thick. (Who'd take the trouble to measure this?)

This was awe-some!

All kinds of topping on the strawberry chocolate.

MNCH MNCH

Wow, there's almond inside!

I had quite a few that were home made. Here are two samples.

I ran out of space to write it in Volume 9, but I wanted to thank you for all the Valentine's Day chocolates! (Come on, that was so long ago!) Thank you so much!

CHAPTER FIFTY-SEVEN
OMINOUS
EYES

AMIBOSHI'S FATHER AND MOTHER! WHAT COULD HAVE--?
MIAKA ...
WH-WHY !?
HURRY! GET THEM INSIDE!
FATHER! MOTHER !
SLAMM
AMI-BOSHI !
IT'S NOT THAT BAD. THEY GOT MY ARM, AND YOUR MOTHER'S ONLY FAINTED.

THIS IS A QU-DONG ARROW! SO THEY DID FIND ME!
WHAT?
I USED MY CHI TO EASE YOUR FEVER.
NAKAGO MUST HAVE DETECTED IT... AND FOUND ME.
NAKAGO!
HE DESTROYED THE VILLAGE!
BUT HE'S NOT AFTER YOU, AMIBOSHI...
HE WANTS ME! NAKAGO REALIZED I WAS HERE!
BUT WHY? HE'S DEFILED ME. I CAN'T SUMMON SUZAKU ANYMORE.

IN ANY CASE, THIS IS TOO MUCH!
ATTACKING INNOCENT VILLAGERS LIKE THIS...
SO YOU *ARE* HERE, PRIESTESS OF SUZAKU!
MIAKA, WAIT! YOU CAN'T GO OUT THERE!
I'M GOING! NAKAGO NEEDS A GOOD PUNCHING OUT!!
YOU WILL COME WITH ME!
STEP BACK, MIAKA! AND... DON'T WATCH THIS!

ARRRGH!!
BURST !!
AAAHH!!

DON'T WORRY. THE SOUND TOOK OUT ONE MAN HIDING AROUND THE CORNER AND TWO OTHERS NEAR THE TREE.
AMI-BOSHI... !!
I FEEL SOMEONE'S CHI... IT'S HUGE!
AMI-BOSHI?
IS THIS... TOMO !?
TAMA-HOME... YOU WILL STAY HERE FOR ALL ETERNITY.
ARE YOU SURPRISED THAT AN ILLUSION TOOK CONTROL OF YOU?

YOU'RE CALLED... TOMO, AREN'T YOU?
DON'T YOU REGRET...
...THAT CLOWN SUIT YOU HAVE ON?
THOSE GAUDY PRIMARY COLORS!
NO SENSE FOR USING MAKEUP!
THOSE FEATHERS ARE SO LAME!
HOW CAN YOU EVEN STEP OUTSIDE IN THAT GET-UP?
THIS WON'T IMPRESS THE GIRLS!
... HEH.
HOW I PITY YOUNG MEN THESE DAYS WITH NO UNDER-STANDING OF TRUE ART.
MY MAKEUP IS SYMBOLIC. INDIGO REPRESENTS STRATEGY. BLACK IS LOYALTY...
...CON-TRASTED AGAINST THE BRIGHT GOLD OF HARMONY...
TOMO, TAMA-HOME TOOK OFF.
HEY!!
SEE YA!!

I CAN'T WASTE MY TIME WITH THAT WEIRDO!
WHAT'S THAT ?
!!
THE LIGHTS OF THE XI-LANG CAPITAL. THE *REAL* XI-LANG.
THE DESERT VERSION, IN WHICH YOUR FRIENDS ARE DYING OF ESPOSURE, IS AN ILLUSION.

MY FRIENDS !?
THEY'LL SOON BE DEAD. NOT AS SOON AS YOU, HOWEVER.
!?
TAMA-HOME !!

MIAKA, TAMA-HOME'S IN TROUBLE!
HE'S VERY CLOSE BY!
NO. I CAN'T GO TO HIM.
WH-WHY!?
...
I CAN'T TELL YOU. BUT I HAVE NO RIGHT TO BE NEAR HIM.
THAT DOESN'T MAKE SENSE! YOU TWO WERE IN *LOVE!!*
YOU *HAVE* TO BE TOGETHER!!
I'LL BRING HIM, OKAY? YOU *WAIT* FOR US HERE, OKAY?
HUAIKE...

Enemy

Here are the details. First, Tamahome. When I found out the meaning for his character was "man with courage," I stopped short! I started looking up the other characters and burst out laughing.
"Nuriko" = graceful beauty.
"Hotohori" = a highly ranked person.
"Tasuki" = help, assistance, protection.
Then, "Chichiri" means home town. "Chiriko" means to widen and spread. "Mitsukake" means to suffer. As for the Seiryu warriors—*Are you even interested?*—I hadn't checked them before so I'll look them up now! *Watase pulls out her Kanji character dictionary.*
"Su" of "Suboshi" = to compete, fight. *Wow!*
"Ami" of "Amiboshi" = go far, cut off.
"Soi" = to draw near, to be wed.
"Tomo" = despicable... Ha ha!
"Ashitare" = back, the end.
"Mi" of "Miboshi" = trash collecting, and...
What the--? Now this is a shock for Watase!! "...sitting cross-legged"!? Those who've been reading FY serialized in the magazine must know how Miboshi has always remained in that sitting position the whole time!! Geez!!
"Nakago" = prudence (strategy, maybe?), center, considerate... hmm. ðð There are a lot of other meanings, but I highlighted the ones that match him.
Oh yeah, my assistant did a reading of Tamahome's name and found that it signified "poverty, looks after others, loses family, gentle in appearance, but strong inside" (wait, isn't it the other way around?) That really took me by surprise. ððð
You might think I'm lying, but this was all a coincidence. Really! I find it a little frightening myself.

The world can work in mysterious ways...!!

TELL ME HOW THE THORNS FEEL.
YOU'LL FEEL MUCH BETTER SOON.
IT'S NOT IN MY NATURE TO CAUSE PAIN.
I'LL MAKE SURE YOU DIE A PLEASURABLE DEATH.
I'M SURPRISED THAT SOI'S APHRODI-SIAC DIDN'T HOLD YOU.
I WENT THROUGH SUCH TROUBLE TO MAKE HER LOOK LIKE YOUR BELOVED.
RRNN!!
HEY, HEY, HEY!!

WH-WHAT IS THIS, YOU PERVERT !?!
HOW WAS IT? THE BODY OF A GIRL YOU CAN NEVER TOUCH NO MATTER YOUR ADORATION.
A MERE RECOLLECTION OF HER WARMTH SETS YOU ON FIRE.
HA HA HAAA!
HA HA HAA.
THE BODY CANNOT LIE.
IT FEELS NICE, DOESN'T IT?
A SIMPLE ILLUSION, BUT ISN'T IT AS SOFT AS THE SKIN OF YOUR PRIESTESS ?
DON'T...
...USE TWISTED WORDS FOR *HER!!*

TAKE IT BACK!!
SHE'S MY--
YOUR "SACRED LOVE"? YOU ARE SO NAÏVE!
I WONDER... SHOULD I DEFILE THAT SACRED LOVE OF YOURS?
!!
IF YOU DO ANYTHING TO MIAKA...
...I'LL *KILL* YOU, YOU BASTARD!!

"WAIT FOR ME HERE!!"
I'M SORRY, AMIBOSHI ...
I HAVE TO SEE YUI AND GET US BOTH BACK TO OUR OWN WORLD!
I *DO* WANT TO SEE TAMAHOME.
BUT I JUST DON'T DESERVE HIM.
YUI AND NAKAGO ARE PROBABLY HEADING TO XI-LANG.
BUT...
...I'M RUNNING *AWAY* FROM TAMAHOME.
!!

SOI !!
AH--
WHERE ARE YOU GOING, PRIESTESS OF SUZAKU?
YOUR BELOVED TAMAHOME ISN'T HERE.
...!? TAMAHOME AND I ARE...
YOU'RE SAYING THAT YOU'RE NOT TOGETHER? THAT'S NOT WHAT *HE* SAYS.

SO YOU SAW HIM!?
HE MAY BE MY ENEMY, BUT HIS COURAGE IMPRESSED ME. HE TOLD ME THAT EVEN IF HOPE IS GONE, WE SHOULD STILL HAVE FAITH.
...
TRUE. I WONDER THE SAME THING.
IF YOU ACTUALLY *HAD* INTER-COURSE WITH NAKAGO...
...WHY... WHY ARE YOU TELLING ME THIS? WHY DON'T YOU KILL ME!?
...I'M CERTAIN I WOULD HAVE KILLED YOU AT FIRST SIGHT.

DOES THAT MEAN... THAT I'M...
WHAT !?
...STILL A VIRGIN !?
TAMAHOME IS FIGHTING FOR HIS LIFE ON THAT CLIFF.
BUT YOU'RE RIGHT. IT'S BEST NOT TO GO.
GASP
TAMA-HOME!
BECAUSE THAT WILL BE THE END OF YOU...

TAMA-HOME!
TAMA-HOME !!
"YOU *HAVE* TO BE TOGETHER!!"
TMP
!!
WHAT A FOOL.
SHE RISKS HERSELF FOR NOTHING MORE THAN A *MAN.*
BUT I MUST ADMIT THAT THE TWO OF YOU...
...BRING OUT THE *ENVY* IN ME.

TAMA-HOME!
PLEASE BE ALL RIGHT!
AAHHHH...
YOU'LL KILL *ME?*
DIDN'T YOU SAY THE SAME WHEN YOU WOUNDED NAKAGO?
WE MUST KEEP YOU FROM SAYING IT AGAIN.
WHAT ARE YOU PLANNING, TOMO!?

!!
BACK AWAY FROM TAMA-HOME *NOW,* TOMO!!
...HUH?
SUBO-SHI...?
NO.
YOU'RE AMIBO-SHI!
SO YOU'RE STILL ALIVE!
GET AWAY FROM HIM OR ELSE!

AMI-BOSHI, WHAT ARE ...
HEH... WHAT DO YOU PLAN ON DOING?
LIKE YOU, I AM A SEIRYU WARRIOR. ARE YOU PLANNING TO *FIGHT* ME?
TAMAHOME!!
はっ
I'M HERE, TAMA-HOME!!

MIAKA !!
OH, NO YOU DON'T !!
!?

GAGH!

HEH!
DID HE THINK I'D SIT STILL FOR HIM?
TAMA-HOME!
...MIAKA...
TAMAHOME!!

TAMA-HOME!!
TAMA-HOME... I'M SO SORRY!
MIAKA... IS IT REALLY YOU...?
....
SQUEEEEEEZ
OWWWWWW!!
TAMA-HOME... NAKAGO NEVER TOUCHED ME!
I CAN STILL SUMMON SUZAKU!

REALLY !?
YES !
THAT'S GREAT.
THAT'S JUST WONDERFUL !!
AMI-BOSHI...
...I FELL AND HURT MY LEG. HE RESCUED ME.
HE SWORE TO BRING YOU BACK. HE DID EVERYTHING HE COULD FOR US.
P-PLEASE FORGIVE MY BETRAYAL AT THE CEREMONY.
....

WHEN WAS THAT AGAIN?
HEY, WE'RE FRIENDS, RIGHT?
!
TAMA-HOME...
AMI-BOSHI!?
TAMA-HOME, WATCH OU--

...UH...
TAMA-
HOME
!!

CHAPTER FIFTY-EIGHT
COUNTERFEIT
MEMORY

TAMA-HOME !!
HA! LET'S NOT GET AHEAD OF OURSELVES. THAT WAS ONLY MY DOUBLE.
DOUBLE... !?
...MI...
...AKA...

R... RUN...!
TAMAHOME!!

TAMA... HOME...
NO...
NOOOOOO!!!
GASP!
MIAKA!! HOLD YOURSELF TOGETHER...
...OR YOU'LL FALL UNDER HIS ILLU-SION!!

OH, NO !!
!!
HA HA! MY SKILLS HAVE TAKEN CONTROL OF YOU, PRIESTESS OF SUZAKU.
WH-WHERE AM I !?
TAMA-HOME... GIVE HIM BACK TO ME!!
IMPOSSIBLE, I'M AFRAID. YOU SAW IT, DID YOU NOT? SAW HIM DIE.

YOU'RE LYING!! HE CAN'T BE DEAD!!
ACCEPT HIS DEATH. AND I WILL TRANSPORT YOU TO A WONDERFUL WORLD!
AND YOU CAN BE GRATEFUL FOR MY KINDNESS.
HA HA HA HA HA HA HA!
WHY ARE YOU PULLING US APART?
WE JUST WANT TO BE WITH EACH OTHER.
WHY!?
GIVE HIM BACK... GIVE HIM...

GIMME BACK MY GUY !!
WOMP
WOMP
GIMME! GIMME! GIMME! GIMME!
MIAKA !
THAT *WAS* THE TEACHER !!
WHAT !?

DINNNGG
DONNNGG
DINNNGG
DONNN

MY... JUNIOR HIGH...
...CLASS ?
DINNNGG
DONNNGG
DINNNGG
DONNNGG
A DREAM... ?
YŪ--
YŪKI!!
A STUDENT WHO FALLS ASLEEP INSTEAD OF STUDYING FOR HER ENTRANCE EXAMS MUST BE EITHER FEARLESS OR JUST STUPID!!
AFTER HOMEROOM, YOU'RE COMING TO THE GUIDANCE COUNSELOR'S OFFICE WITH ME!! GOT THAT !?
YEAH, I GOT IT.
I'M SORRY, SIR!
BOW
WHAMM
YŪKI!!
HA HA AA
HA AA HA HA AA
IDIOT.

HAA HAA HAA HA
YŪKI, YOU'RE SUCH A SPAZ!
YOU KNOW HE'S THE ONE TEACHER YOU SHOULDN'T GET TICKED OFF!
HAAA HAA
"GIMME BACK MY GUY??" WHAT KIND OF DREAM WAS THAT?
.....
I DON'T REMEM-BER.
SO MUCH FOR TEACHER RECOMMEN-DATIONS GETTING INTO HIGH SCHOOL.
COME ON, YUI! DON'T SCARE ME!
.....?

LOOK AT *HIM!*
I DON'T REMEMBER HIM IN MY CLASS!
WELL, PRIESTESS OF SUZAKU?
MY SHELL INCORPORATED YOUR MIND AND CHI AND FORMED THIS ILLUSION OUT OF YOUR MEMORIES.
I MUST SAY, THE PRIESTESSES CAME FROM AN EXTRA-ORDINARY WORLD.
I'LL HAVE MY SHELL MEMORIZE IT AND SHOW NAKAGO LATER.

Now to change the subject. Here, something I read in your recent fan mail. It says that "Fushigi Yūgi" graphic novels and merchandise showed up on TV in Hanakin Dataland. I didn't know about it at all and didn't watch the series. My editors didn't know about it either! Meanwhile, my '94 calendar showed up all the time in the TV drama Tanin no Fukō wa Mitsu no Aji ("The Delicious Woes of Others") which made me happy! It was a while ago.
By the way, the second CD book will be released on August 3. This time, it is amazing, if I do say so myself. First of all, there are so many voice actors. 14 actors. 14!! There are the leads Noriko Hidaka (Miaka), Toshihiko Seki (Tamahome), Wakana Yamazaki (Yui), Yasunori Matsumoto (Hotohori), Minami Takayama (Nuriko), Rin Mizuhara (Tai Yi-Jun)!! Then on top of that, Kazuki Yao (Tasuki), Kappei Yamaguchi (Chichiri), Megumi Origasa (Chiriko), Jurota Osugi (Mitsukake), Tetsuya Iwanaga (Amiboshi), and Ryutaro Okiayu (Nakago) were in it. Eiji Yanagisawa and Toru Furusawa gave a fierce (so fierce it terrified me) performance as the men attacking Yui. I was so impressed I had to write them all down!! My right hand's trembling. What a terrific cast!! Tremble, tremble! They're all on the same recording! What a great deal. I actually visited a recording session at the studio... but given my origins as an anime fan, I completely lost control, went haywire, lost my mind, went nuts, etc.

OH, BOY!
OH, BOY!
OH, BOY!
OH, BOY!

THE WORLD INSIDE...
...THE PRIESTESSES' SWEET DREAM...
YES. I APOLOGIZE FOR MY BEHAVIOR.
ARE YOU FINALLY AWAKE, YŪKI?
BY THE WAY...
生活指導室
COUNSELOR'S OFFICE
YOUR FIRST CHOICE WAS JONAN HIGH SCHOOL, RIGHT?
OH, NO!
"YOUR CHANCES WERE SLIM TO START, BUT NOW..."
......
......
......

I KNOW THAT YOUR GRADES CAN GET YOU INTO ANY SCHOOL YOU WANT, BUT...
EH!?
...THAT'S NO EXCUSE TO TAKE YOUR STUDIES LIGHTLY.
I-I'M SORRY... COULD YOU REPEAT THAT!?
THAT'S NO EXCUSE TO--
NO! I MEAN, BEFORE THAT!
YOUR GRADES CAN GET YOU INTO ANY SCHOOL YOU WANT.
?
WHY DIDN'T YOU TELL ME SOONER!?!
HURRAH
JAPAN'S NO. 1
I'VE TOLD YOU THAT FOR YEARS.
THANK YOU, SIR!
I DIDN'T *KNOW*!

I'M GETTING INTO JONAN HIGH SCHOOL!
AND I THOUGHT I MIGHT ONLY SQUEAK BY!
WHATTA RELIEF!
MIAKA !
I THOUGHT YOU'D GET CHEWED OUT FOR SURE. BUT YOU'RE SMILING!
HERE'S YOUR COAT AND BAG.
YOU WAITED FOR ME?
HEY! HOW ABOUT WE GET A BITE TO EAT.
WHOO-HOOO! ODDLY, I'M HUNGRY TODAY.
ODDLY, YOU'RE HUNGRY ALL THE TIME.

MIAKA, ARE YOU OKAY !?
MY HEAD! IF I GET ANY DUMBER, SOMEBODY'S GONNA PAY!
DON'T WORRY! YOU *CAN'T* GET ANY DUMBER !
AONO !
THIS BOY!!
LOOK, I'M REALLY SORRY! LET'S GO SEE THE NURSE!
EH? BUT...
I'M SORRY !!
ARE YOU ALL RIGHT !?
SEE YOU, MIAKA. WE'LL JUST HEAD ON HOME.
GRIN GRIN

HUH! WHY !?
IDIOT! YOU WANT US TO DO THIS!
WHSPR
YOU'VE LIKED THIS GUY FOREVER, RIGHT? THIS IS YOUR CHANCE!
GO FOR IT!
ドキ…
"LIKED"...? OH, I GUESS I HAVE.
LET'S GO.
THIS PAST YEAR EVER SINCE WE BECAME CLASSMATES, I'VE HAD A CRUSH ON HIM...
保健室
NURSE'S OFFICE
ドキ ドキ
ドキ ドキ
YOU'VE GOT A LITTLE BUMP. DO YOU FEEL SICK?
THE BALL HIT YOU PRETTY HARD.

YUI SAID IT WAS MY CHANCE.
O-OH, I'M FINE. I GUESS I LOOK A LITTLE LIKE A GOAL POST.
WHAT DOES THAT MEAN?
MAYBE IT'S TIME I QUIT THE SOCCER CLUB...
...LOOK WHAT IT DID TO YOU!
EH?
YOU'RE TAKING EXAMS FOR JONAN HIGH SCHOOL, RIGHT?
I AM, TOO.
YOU SEE, SINCE YOU'RE GOING THERE...
...I'M TRYING FOR THE SAME SCHOOL.
WHAT?
D-DOES THAT MEAN...
WOW-EEE-EEE!

I WANTED TO WAIT UNTIL WE BOTH PASSED THE EXAMS AND GOT IN...
...BUT I LIKE YOU.
AND I'D REALLY LIKE YOU TO GO OUT WITH ME.
WHAAAAT!?
HA HA...
THAT IS SO SWEET.
TOMO !!

WHAT ARE YOU DOING TO HER!?
HA HA... THIS TECHNIQUE IS OF A DIFFERENT ORDER THAN WHAT I USED ON THE CELESTIAL WARRIORS.
I HAVE SEALED AWAY, NOT ONLY HER MIND, BUT HER BODY AS WELL.
HAVE YOU FORGOTTEN HOW I CAN CREATE NUMEROUS ILLUSIONARY DOUBLES? THEY ARE, IN FACT, ME.
AND ONE OF ME WILL BE THE ONE TO TAKE HER VIR-GINITY.
IT'S TRUE... I DISLIKE FORCING THE WILL OF WOMEN IN THIS WAY, BUT...
MMBL MMBL
M-- MIAKA...
...WILL NEVER BE FOOLED BY YOUR TRICKS!!

AMI-BOSHI... YOU *ARE* NAIVE, AREN'T YOU?
A WOMAN WHO HAS JUST WITNESSED THE MURDER OF HER BELOVED WILL DO ANYTHING TO ESCAPE AN UNBEARABLE REALITY.
THIS HAPPY FANTASY WAS SOUGHT BY THE PRIESTESS HERSELF.
DID YOU REALLY HAVE TO DRAG ME ALL THE WAY OUT HERE?
DON'T BLAME ME! YOU'RE THE ONE WHO USED UP ALL OF THE HERB!
THE ONLY PLACE IT GROWS IS UNDER THE BUDDHA STATUE!
IT GETS TOO HOT TO LOOK DURING THE DAY.
HM? LOOK OVER THERE...

HEY, ARE YOU ALL RIGHT!!
UN NH ...
GOOD, HE'S ALIVE !
...MI...
...AKA...
WOW! YOU MADE ALL MY FAVORITE DISHES!!
WELL, YOUR GRADES ON YOUR PRACTICE TEST WERE SO GOOD.
YAY !
JUST KEEP UP THE GOOD WORK.

QUADRATIC EQUATIONS STUMPED ME IN CRAM SCHOOL, BUT I BREEZED RIGHT THROUGH THEM. EVEN THE *TEACHER* WAS NICE.
YOU ALL COULD LEARN A THING OR TWO FROM YŪKI!
I REALLY WANTED TO GO TO YOTSUBADAI, BUT I'M A SHOO-IN FOR JONAN! SO, IT'S ALL GOOD.
YUI'S GOING THERE... AND NOW, SO WILL AONO.
"I LIKE YOU."
BEH HEH HEH HEH
HEH HEH HEH
MIAKA, YOU'RE FLAVORING YOUR STEW WITH DROOL.
WHAT A GREAT DAY TO PUT IN MY DIARY!
"AONO, THE GUY I'VE ALWAYS LIKED, SAID TODAY THAT HE LIKED ME!!"

THIS FEELS LIKE A DREAM.
YOU CAN GIVE ME AN ANSWER NEXT TIME.
I'LL BE SO EMBARRASSED NEXT TIME I SEE HIM...
HUH ?
WHAT'S AONO'S FIRST NAME?
THAT'S WEIRD. I CAN'T REMEM- BER.
AH! IT'S SO LATE! I GOTTA START STUDYING!
OH... LOOK AT THIS MESS!

OH ...
鬼
鬼 常 おに
キ
Oni, Ki, Demon
鬼
2. Constellation name. One of the 28 constellations of Chinese astrology. Tamahome.
WHAT?
WHY IS MY...
...HEART BEATING SO FAST?

THERE'S A HUGE LUMP IN MY THROAT!
WHY !?
Tamahome.
MAYBE I JUST NEED SOME AIR...
...AND I'LL CALM DOWN.
カラ
!

AONO!
パッ
キィ
AONO!? WHAT IS IT?
I HAD A QUICK QUESTION. UH, DON'T SLIP ON THE ICE THERE...
OR... MAKE A NOTE OF IT FOR NEXT TIME.

MY OLDER BROTHER... USED THIS PENCIL TO PASS HIS ENTRANCE EXAMS. IT'S GOOD LUCK.
!
I THOUGHT YOU SHOULD HAVE IT.
YOU CAME ALL THE WAY...
...IN THE SNOW TO GIVE THIS TO ME?
I COULD'VE WAITED UNTIL SCHOOL TOMOR-ROW...
...BUT I WANTED TO SEE YOUR FACE.
THAT'S IT. SORRY TO INTERRUPT YOUR STUDIES.
SEE YOU TOMORROW.
AONO...
...YOU REALLY CARE FOR ME.

鬼
ブンブン
UM...
HEY...
YOU CAN...
...ASK ME OUT ANY TIME.

... REALLY ?
ARE YOU SURE !?
YES... I MEAN, I LIKE YOU TOO.
THAT'S *GREAT* !!
I REALLY DO LIKE YOU.
ドキ ドキ ドキ
AND NOW, I'LL NEVER LET GO.
ME TOO.

...AONO...

HA HA... THIS IS TOO MUCH!
... MIAKA.
WAKE UP, MIAKA!!
YOU HAVE TO REMEMBER TAMA-HOME!!
HAH! THAT WON'T DO ANY GOOD.
CAN I CALL YOU BY YOUR FIRST NAME?

YOU CAN CALL ME "TOMO."
TOMO... ?
YES.
MY NAME'S TOMO.
YOUR SOUL AND BODY WILL BE MINE.
AND YOU WILL BE TRAPPED IN THIS SHELL FOR ETERNITY.

SPECIAL STRIP
What's So Fushigi about Fushigi Yūgi, Special Edition

There must be dojinshi like this! ☺ I heard there was one for Tasuki and Nuriko. *I'd like to see it!*

What's So Fushigi About Fushigi Yūgi #2

Hey, the name keeps on changing!

Q1: I know Miaka has spare clothes, but what is Yui doing about her clothes?
A: Yui has very nimble fingers. I'm sure she can sew her own underwear using silk-like fabrics! She probably has her uniform washed every night.

Q2: Is Tomo gay? I mean the outfit...
A: Yep. (To be blunt.) Tomo is homosexual. Furthermore, he's in love with Nakago! ☺ His criticisms of Nakago may be an expression of love. "Why," you ask. He just ended up this way. Those of you who know Chinese opera might've realized that I had the opera in mind for his character. The feathers are also from it. In fact, they might be even more gaudy in the actual opera.
After I first drew Tomo, I saw "Farewell My Concubine," and there was that scene where the female impersonator lead is in love with the male protagonist during the performance of "Front and Back." Which might make you think, "so it's a movie about gay guys." No, not at all!! The drama's much deeper than that. What a great movie! *Really!* Then there was also "M Butterfly" (about a man who doesn't realize the woman he falls for is in fact a man), and then this Chinese opera...

Personally, a gay theme is no different from a straight theme for me. Those factors were simply in the atmosphere when I came up with Tomo. But ever since Fushigi began, assistant after assistant would not stop talking about it! ☺ With characters like this, I guess it's only natural. *What does ya thinks, Olive Oyl?* I guess everyone just got into it.
And so Tomo got his look and personality. By the way, I had the same kind of question with regard to Nakago (refer to left comic). Although he isn't gay, he wouldn't let gender stand in his way if he is attracted to someone. It seems natural if you think of it as attraction between people rather than attraction between the sexes.
That's what I thought after seeing "Farewell My Concubine."

CHAPTER FIFTY-NINE
COUNTERFEIT
LOVE

WHAT!?
SO YOU'RE GOING OUT?
WITH AONO?
HE'S THE GUY ALL THE GIRLS ARE CHASING! ARE YOU *SERIOUS,* MIAKA!?
HA HA! YUP!
YEAH, AND... ACTUALLY, THERE'S MORE TO IT.
?
SEE...
YOU'RE MAKING US ILL, SPIT IT OUT!

Enemy

And because of that... I was so nervous I started sweating! (My entire body was drenched!) My voice broke. Blood rushed to my head. I almost fainted. I just totally clammed up... **and couldn't even talk to them!! *Dammit!!*** *It was so sad and pathetic. I really missed my chance!*
I couldn't even look at them. Why am I so shy!? Argh!! If I could only be more social!! B-but, no!! Readers who know anime and voice actors must know what I'm talking about!! I mean voice actors are like super stars!!!
I would recall the voice of the character from the anime that I watched all through high school, and I'd realize, "S-so this person did..." There was no way I could start up a conversation. But finally a reporter from Animate arranged for a short interview with myself along with Mr. Seki, Mr. Matsumoto, Ms. Hidaka, and Ms. Yamazaki... "Wow, we're actually breathing the same air in the same room!" Am I a sickie or WHAT!? ☺ I actually sat next to Ms. Hidaka! She actually shook my hand. She actually shook my hand!! Pant, pant, pant. *She seemed so cheerful and kind.*
She and Ms. Yamazaki told me they had bought my graphic novels, and I almost burst out crying. Sniff, sniff... But I was so shy, I couldn't watch and had my back to them. I'm such an idiot! (During the entire time they were recording!) That's right! I hear that if you send in the survey form that comes with the CD, you'll get an autographed sign card with the signatures of all 12 voice actors and Yū Watase! Really!? They must be copies... One of them might be real! (I have one displayed in my room!♫) *I'm acting like a junior-high-school girl!!*

H-HE...
...KISSED ME!
UMMM...
MIAKA, YOU'RE BAD!
SOME EXAM STUDENT YOU ARE!
YOU DON'T DESERVE BOYFRIEND BLISS!!
?
...MIAKA!

GOOD MORNING!
G- GOOD MORNING!
TOMO!
MIAKA, GOOD MORNING!
YOU KNOW, WE NEVER FINISHED LAST NIGHT'S KISS!!
HUGG
BUT WE MUSTN'T, TOMO! NOT HERE AT SCHOOL!
NO!! YOU TWO ARE SUCH PERVERTS!!
STOP IT, ALREADY!!

AHEM
ALL KIDDING ASIDE, I'M GLAD YOU BOTH FEEL THE SAME WAY.
Y-YEAH... THANKS, YUI.
3-4
TIME FOR JAPANESE-LIT STUDY HALL.
ANYBODY STUDYING FOR THE ENTRANCE EXAMS, GRAB A DICTIONARY AND MEMORIZE.
MY LUCKY DAY! GIVE ME THE KANJI DICTIONARY!
I'M COOL. I GOT MY WORKBOOK.
IS THIS BECAUSE MR. TAKAGI'S LATE FOR CLASSES *AGAIN?*
HE'S GOT TO GET IT TOGETHER!
HEY! SOMEONE'S ALWAYS WRITING NOTES IN THESE SCHOOL DICTIONARIES TO LOOK ON A CERTAIN PAGE!
HA HA HA HA HA!
YEAH, AND THAT PAGE ALWAYS HAS SOME DIRTY WORD!
OH! HERE'S ONE. "LOOK UP PAGE 581!"
FLIP FLIP FLIP FLIP
SO SERIOUS...

THANK GOODNESS FOR STUDY HALL TODAY. MR. TAKAGI'S SUCH A DRAG! HE ALWAYS MAKES ME DO THE READING.
EVERY-THING'S GOING THE WAY I WANT IT TO GO...
FLIP FLIP
FLIP
鬼
THERE IT IS AGAIN!
FLIP FLIP FLIP
WHY IS MY HEART RACING?
Tamahome Constellation. The name of a star constellation in ancient Chinese astrology.
The four gods of the north, south, east and west (Genbu, Suzaku, Seiryu and Byakko respectively) are assigned seven star constellations each.
Genbu
Seiryu
Suzaku
Byakko
TAMA-HOME IS ONE OF THE CONSTEL-LATIONS OF THE SOUTH GOD SUZAKU...

PAPP
MIAKA!
WHAT IS GOING ON HERE?
SOUTH GOD SUZAKU? A SUZAKU CONSTEL-LATION?
I TOLD YOU TO CUT IT OUT!!
AAAAAH!
LET'S STUDY TO-GETHER.
OH!
UMM, MIAKA?
MY FIRST KISS.
I KNEW I'D BE EMBAR-RASSED SEEING HIM AFTER WHAT HAPPENED YESTERDAY...
OKI
DOKI
DOKI
DOKI
DOKI

TOMORROW IS SUNDAY... WHY DON'T YOU COME OVER TO MY HOUSE?
HUH?
IT'S OKAY, ISN'T IT?
N-NO, TOMO!! THERE'S *DANGER* IN WHAT YOU SUGGEST!
AFTER YESTER-DAY, WHAT DO YOU EXPECT WITH THAT INVITA-TION?
MIAKA, YOUR HUGE GRIN DOESN'T FIT WITH YOUR FACE.
I MEAN, WE'RE TRYING TO PASS EXAMS FOR THE SAME SCHOOL. WE SHOULD STUDY TOGETHER.
"STUDY" !?
WHAT WERE YOU THINKING ?
I WASN'T THINKING ANYTHING... MUMBLE, MUMBLE.

SO IT'S A PROMISE, RIGHT, MIAKA?
THAT'S RIGHT... NOW YOU WILL SURRENDER YOURSELF TO MY ILLUSIONARY DOUBLE.
.....
AMIBOSHI, YOU DON'T HAVE A PRAYER OF RESCUING HER FROM INSIDE SHEN... INSIDE MY SHELL.
YOU HAVEN'T THE POWER TO FOIL MY TECH-NIQUES.

NO POWER AT ALL!
AHH...
UN NH...
MI... ...AKA.
HUFF HUFF
HOW IS HE?
WELL, DEAR, THE THING IS...
URRR--

...HE ISN'T INJURED VERY BADLY. HE JUST TOOK A LIGHT BLOW.
TRULY? THAT'S A MIRACLE, GIVEN HOW HE FELL FROM THE CLIFF.
THE TALL GRASS BELOW MUST HAVE SAVED HIM.
BUT IT'S NOT RIGHT! HE SEEMS TO BE IN A LOT OF PAIN.
LET ME HAVE A LOOK!
HEY, YOUNG MAN! WHERE DOES IT HURT?
B-- BEEN STABBED...
...MY BACK...
...BLEED-ING...
THAT EXPLAINS IT.
THEN I'LL PUT YOU OUT OF YOUR MISERY.

...MIAKA...
?
WH-
WHERE
AM I
!?
CALM DOWN. YOU'RE IN MY HOUSE. YOU WERE IN THE THROWS OF ILLUSION. I BROKE IT WITH ACUPRESSURE.
NO MORE MISERY, RIGHT.
!?
GOOD, YOU'RE ALL RIGHT NOW.
YOU MEAN, THAT WAS ILLUSION?
DAMMIT! HE TRICKED ME!!

MAYBE IT WAS A TRICK, BUT NORMALLY YOU'D HAV DIED OF SHOCK THE AND THERE.
THE FACT THAT YOU CAN TAKE THE PAIN MUST MEAN YOU'RE A SUZAKU WARRIOR. EH, TAMAHOME ?
H-HOW DO YOU KNOW MY NAME?
DON'T YOU REMEMBER ME?
YOU'VE GROWN QUITE A BIT OVER THE PAST EIGHT YEARS, BUT YOU HAVEN'T CHANGED THAT MUCH!
!!
MA-- MASTER !?

I NEVER THOUGHT I'D BE INVITED OVER SO SOON. I'LL HAVE TO WATCH MYSELF AROUND HIS FAMILY.
LET'S SEE... I HAVE THE PENCIL HE GAVE ME...
MY, I'VE NEVER SEEN SUCH A CHARMING, POLITE YOUNG WOMAN!
YES, YOU'LL BE THE PERFECT BRIDE!
FATHER
MOTHER
DON'T! YOU FLATTER ME!
OH, PLEASE STOP! YOU'RE MAKING ME BLUSH!
.....
SENILITY HITS SO YOUNG!
I-I'M SORRY. I DIDN'T REALIZE YOU WERE HERE!
THAT'S ALL RIGHT! HEY, I KNOW A SHORTCUT PAST THE LIBRARY...

CITY CENTRAL LIBRA
WHAT'S WRONG ?
I'VE BEEN... HERE BEFORE.
...? SURE YOU HAVE. ME, TOO. EVERYBODY'S BEEN HERE.
CITY CEN
I CAME HERE... WITH YUI ONCE...
SOMETHING... VERY IMPORTANT HAPPENED HERE...
YOU'RE JUST IMAGINING THINGS. LET'S GO.
THERE'S SOME *CAKE* AT MY HOUSE WAITING FOR YOU.
COUNT ME IN !!

IS IT JUST MY IMAGINATION?
SOMETHING FEELS AWFULLY STRANGE HERE...
THANKS FOR THE HOSPI-TALITY!
스스
HUH? ISN'T ANYONE HERE ?
COME ON IN.
WOW! YOUR ROOM'S SO NICE AND CLEAN. MY BROTHER'S IS A MESS.
I'M NOT A FAN OF... DIS-ORDER.

HMM.
HEY!
YOU CAN SEE THE LIBRARY FROM HERE.
WHY DOES IT BOTHER ME SO MUCH? WHAT HAPPENED THERE?
THAT "DEMON" CHARACTER, SUZAKU, THE LIBRARY...
HEY, TOMO! LET'S GO TO THE LIBRARY LATER. I WANT TO LOOK SOME-THING UP.
AH...

WHA--
WHA-AAAA-AAT!?
RRMM!
TH-- THIS CAN'T BE--
...THE WAY I GET MY FIRST TASTE OF THE *ADULT WORLD!?*
N-NO! IT'S ALL TOO SUDDEN!!
H-- HOLD ON!!
WHY? WE'RE IN LOVE, AREN'T WE?
B-BUT YOU SAID WE WERE GOING TO STUDY! WE'RE STILL IN JUNIOR HIGH. WHAT WILL YOUR *FAMILY* SAY?
FAMILY? I HAVE NO FAMILY HERE...
WE'RE ALL ALONE.

OH...
I LOVE YOU. I'VE LOVED YOU FOR SO LONG.
THIS IS ALL I CAN DO!
OR... ARE YO SAYIN YOU DON' LIKE M
N-NO! THAT'S NOT WHAT I MEAN!!
VERY WELL.

ドクン ドクン ドクン
THERE'S NOTHING TO BE AFRAID OF.
I LIKE TOMO.
THAT MEANS THIS IS OKAY, RIGHT?
ドクン ドクン ドクン!
BUT THERE'S SOMETHING IN MY HEART THAT'S HOLDING ME BACK...
IS THERE OMETHING MPORTANT THAT I'VE ORGOTTEN?

OH, YEAH, THE LIBRARY.
CITY CENTRAL LIBRARY
I HAVE TO REMEMBER! WHAT HAPPENED THERE ?
PEOPLE AREN'T ALLOWED IN THE RESTRICTED PRIVATE LIBRARY.
HEY! LOOK AT THIS, YUI!
"READ TO THE STORY'S END; THE SPELL SHALL GRANT YOUR WISH."

TOMO! I WENT TO THE LIBRARY WITH YUI!
WE FOUND AN OLD BOOK IN THE RESTRICTED PRIVATE LIBRARY!
WE GOT SUCKED INTO THE BOOK SOMEHOW... WHAT WAS ITS NAME... ?
"SUCKED INTO A BOOK?" YOU'RE REMEMBERING SOME DREAM. THINGS LIKE THAT DON'T HAPPEN!
FORGET ABOUT IT.
!
A DREAM... SO IT WAS... A DREAM.
BUT I REMEMBER THE WORLD OF THE BOOK. IT WAS A PLACE LIKE ANCIENT CHINA.

THERE WAS A KING I THIS HUGE PALAC HE WAS AN EMPERO
"WILL YOU SUMMON SUZAKU AND PROTECT OUR EMPIRE, MIAKA?"
"PRIESTESS OF SUZAKU."
"ANY WISH WILL BE GRANTED YO ONCE SUZAK IS SUMMONED THE ONLY ON WITH THAT POWER IS TH PRIESTESS..."
"I COULD GET INTO WHATEVER SCHOOL I WANT TO..."
"I'LL DO IT. I'LL BE THE PRIESTESS OF SUZAKU!!"

PRIESTESS... OF SUZAKU...
THE NAME OF THE EMPEROR WAS... "I, HOTOHORI..."
"...AND THE REST OF THE SEVEN CONSTELLATIONS MUST PROTECT THE PRIESTESS."
"OUR ENEMY, QU-DONG, IS ALSO LOOKING FOR THEIR PRIESTESS. BY SUMMONING THE GOD SEIRYU, THEY SEEK TO RULE HONG-NAN."
"YUI HAS BECOME THE ENEMY. THE PRIESTESS OF SEIRYU."

LET GO OF ME. THIS ISN'T RIGHT!
"BY OBTAINING TREASURES, THE SHENTSO-PAO, IN THE COUNTRIES OF BEI-JIA AND XI-LANG, WE CAN SUMMON SUZAKU."
"YOU MUSTN'T LET THE SHENTSO-PAO FALL INTO THE HANDS OF THE SEIRYU WARRIORS AND THEIR PRIES-TESS."
I'M... *STILL* IN THE BOOK!
AND... *YOU'RE* NOT THE ONE I LOVE!
"SUMMON SUZAKU AND WISH TO BECOME A PART OF THIS WORLD!"
"THEN WE CAN BE TOGETHER."

"TOGETHER FOREVER... MIAKA!"
TAMA-HOME !
TAMAHOME!!

!?
IMPRESSIVE. YOU MANAGED TO DEFEAT THE TECHNIQUE OF THE SEIRYU WARRIOR TOMO!
NOW, YOU SHALL *NEVER* LEAVE THIS WORLD!

ONCE YOU LOSE YOUR VIRGINITY YOU WON'T BE ABLE TO SUMMON SUZAKU. SOMETHING SAVED YOU FROM NAKAGO, BUT THIS TIME THE RESULTS WILL BE DIFFERENT!
HA HA HA!
GASP
TOMO'S ENTIRELY FOCUSED ON HIS SHELL.
IF I'M GONNA ESCAPE, IT'S GOTTA BE NOW!!
THESE VINES ARE ILLUSION. I HAVE TO WAKE MYSELF UP!

YAAAAAHH!!
YOU BAD GUY! STOP IT!! YOU LETCH! YOU DIRTY OLD MAN!!
YOU SPEW A LOT OF INSULTS. CAN'T YOU LET OUT SOME OF THOSE SEDUC-TIVE MOANS?
ASK YOUR BOY-FRIEND. HE KNEW WHAT SOUNDS GOT ME AROUSED!
NO! TAMA-HOME!
HOW CAN I ESCAPE THIS WORLD?

AMI-BOSHI !?
HOW DID YOU ...
MIAKA !
I WILL GIVE YOU POWER TO BREAK THROUGH THE ILLUSION!!

A FLUTE!
HIS HAIR HAS LOOSENED ITS GRIP!
!
!!

...UH...
AAAARRRHH!!
SHEN!!

AH!
MIAKA!! ARE YOU ALL RIGHT !?
MEOW WW!
STAND ASIDE, AMI-BOSHI !

YOU ARE A SEIRYU CELESTIAL WARRIOR.
YOU WOULD RESCUE YOUR ENEMY, THE PRIESTESS OF SUZAKU, BY BETRAYING YOUR COMRADE?
MIAKA MADE ME REALIZE THAT I WAS JUST RUNNING AWAY.
SHE TAUGHT ME THAT I HAVE TO *FIGHT* EVIL.
AND TAMAHOME TREATED ME, HIS ENEMY, AS A FRIEND!
I WON'T LET YOU TOUCH HER!
IT'S *YOU* THAT I'M GOING TO FIGHT!

GIVEN THE STATE OF YOUR FINGERS, YOUR FLUTE WON'T PUT ME IN MUCH DANGER.
HEH!
I SEE. AS YOU WISH.
AND ONCE THE TRAITOR IS PROPERLY COOKED, I'LL TURN MY TASTES TO THE SWEET PRIESTESS OF SUZAKU!
MIAKA! NOW'S THE TIME TO RUN!!
HURRY! YOU HAVE TO WAKE UP!!
MIAKA!!
TO BE CONTINUED IN VOLUME 11: VETERAN

ABOUT THE AUTHOR

Yuu Watase was born on March 5 in a town near Osaka, Japan, and she was raised there before moving to Tokyo to follow the dream of creating manga. In the decade since her debut short story, ***Pajama de Ojama*** ("An Intrusion in Pajamas"), she has produced more than 50 compiled volumes of short stories and continuing series. Her latest series ***Zettai Kareshi*** ("He'll Be My Boyfriend"), is currently running in the anthology magazine ***Shôjo Comic***. Watase's long-running horror/romance story ***Ceres: Celestial Legend*** and her most recently completed series, ***Alice 19th***, are now available in North America published by VIZ. She loves science fiction, fantasy and comedy.

MEET JIMMY KUDO.

Ace high-school student with keen powers of observation, he helps police solve the baffling crimes . . . until, hot on the trial of a suspect, he's accosted and fed a strange chemical which transforms him into a puny grade schooler!

maison ikkoku

THE UNMISSABLE NEW GOLLANCZ MANGA SERIES STARTS HERE!

Yusaku's attempts to study get off to a bad start when he falls head-over-heels for the new manager, and he's a long, long way from winning her heart. For Kyoko already has somebody else on her mind . . . a mysterious "Mr. Soichiro" . . .

VOLUMES 1-4 OUT NOW!

COMPLETE OUR SURVEY AND LET US KNOW WHAT YOU THINK!

❏ Please do NOT send me information about Gollancz Manga, or other Orion titles, products, news and events, special offers or other information.

Name: ______________________

Address: ______________________

Town: __________ County: __________ Postcode: __________

❏ Male ❏ Female Date of Birth (dd/mm/yyyy): __/__/____
(under 13? Parental consent required)

What race/ethnicity do you consider yourself? (please check one)

❏ Asian ❏ Black ❏ Hispanic
❏ White/Caucasian ❏ Other: __________

Which Gollancz Manga series did you purchase?

❏ Case Closed ❏ Dragon Ball ❏ Flame of Recca ❏ Fushigi Yûgi
❏ Maison Ikkoku ❏ One Piece ❏ Rurouni Kenshin ❏ Yu-Gi-Oh!
❏ Yu-Gi-Oh! Duelist

What other Gollancz Manga series have you tried?

❏ Case Closed ❏ Dragon Ball ❏ Flame of Recca ❏ Fushigi Yûgi
❏ Maison Ikkoku ❏ One Piece ❏ Rurouni Kenshin ❏ Yu-Gi-Oh!
❏ Yu-Gi-Oh! Duelist

How many anime and/or manga titles have you purchased in the last year?
How many were Gollancz Manga titles?

Anime	Manga	GM
❏ None	❏ None	❏ None
❏ 1-4	❏ 1-4	❏ 1-4
❏ 5-10	❏ 5-10	❏ 5-10
❏ 11+	❏ 11+	❏ 11+

Reason for purchase: (check all that apply)

❑ Special Offer ❑ Favourite title ❑ Gift

❑ In store promotion If so please indicate which store: ______________________

❑ Recommendation ❑ Other ______________________

Where did you make your purchase?

❑ Bookshop ❑ Comic Shop ❑ Music Store

❑ Newsagent ❑ Video Game Store ❑ Supermarket

❑ Other: ______________ ❑ Online: ______________

What kind of manga would you like to read?

❑ Adventure ❑ Comic Strip ❑ Fantasy

❑ Fighting ❑ Horror ❑ Mystery

❑ Romance ❑ Science Fiction ❑ Sports

❑ Other: ______________________

Which do you prefer?

❑ Sound effects in English

❑ Sound effects in Japanese with English captions

❑ Sound effects in Japanese only with a glossary at the back

Want to find out more about Manga?

Look it up at www.orionbooks.co.uk, or www.viz.com

THANK YOU!

Please send the completed form to:

Manga Survey
Orion Books
Orion House
5 Upper St Martin's Lane
London, WC2H 9EA

All information provided will be used for internal purposes only.
We promise not to sell or otherwise divulge your details.

NO PURCHASE NECESSARY. Requests not in compliance with all terms of this form will not be acknowledged or returned. All submissions are subject to verification and become property of Gollancz Manga.